Overcoming
LIFE'S TRAUMA

Find Closure to the Abuse, Tragedies, and Suffering of Life

Ben S. Howard

Overcoming Life's Trauma
Ben S. Howard

© Copyright 2007-2011 Lifeline Media, LLC

All rights reserved.

No part of this book may be reproduced or transmitted in any form by any means, electronic or mechanical, including photocopying, recording or by any information storage and retrieval system, without specific written permission from the publisher. The scanning, uploading, and distribution of this book via the Internet or via any other means without the permission of the publisher is illegal and punishable by law. Please purchase only authorized electronic editions, and do not participate in or encourage electronic piracy of copyrighted materials.

Lifeline Media, LLC
www.lifeline.com

Book design by Paul Killpack, Highland, Utah

Library of Congress Cataloging-in-Publication Data: Pending

Howard, Ben S.
Overcoming Life's Trauma

Library of Congress Control Number: 2011938590

ISBN: 9781937521103

To Janine, Matthew, and Esther—
you are loved and missed!

Table of Contents

Chapter 1	*The Beginning*	1
Chapter 2	*The Boy*	3
Chapter 3	*The Call*	11
Chapter 4	*Your Story*	19
Chapter 5	*The Force*	31
Chapter 6	*Spiritual Communications*	37
Chapter 7	*Give it Back*	43
Chapter 8	*Justification*	47
Chapter 9	*Pain*	53
Chapter 10	*Universal Law*	59
Chapter 11	*The Nature of Injury*	65
Chapter 12	*Categories*	71
Chapter 13	*Vicarious Injuries*	73
Chapter 14	*Incidental Injuries*	79
Chapter 15	*Unintentional Injuries*	85
Chapter 16	*The Meadow*	95
Chapter 17	*Intentional Injuries*	103
Chapter 18	*The Return*	117
Chapter 19	*Ongoing and Future Injuries*	125
Chapter 20	*The Unexpected Gift*	129
Chapter 21	*A Word of Warning*	135
Chapter 22	*A Note from the Author*	137

Chapter 1

The Beginning

The knowledge in this book has the power to alter the course of your life forever. There are no mystical secrets to be found here. There is no magical formula or trick. It is much more basic than that. In these pages you will find simple, *Universal Truths* that when applied, bring more freedom and joy than can be imagined.

No matter how pure the intent or how important the topic, I believe that sharing *what to do* without actually sharing *how to do it* is a disservice and a frustration to the receiver. I can't tell you how many times I have sat and listened to some teacher tell me all the things I should or should not be doing, without offering the slightest insight on how. That being considered, this book is a *working* book. It will require your effort and participation as we go through the process of learning, experiencing, and applying the principles presented in these pages. With that in mind, let us turn to the topic at hand.

The things that happen to us in life affect us all. We suffer loss, neglect, abandonment, betrayal, abuse, violence, and every other imaginable injury and trauma. These traumas become part of our being, and they affect every part of our spiritual, emotional and physical life.

The purpose of this book is to help you better understand these injuries and traumas and, more specifically, why we have so much trouble letting them go. You will gain the knowledge, skills and understanding necessary to overcome these hurts of life, as well as having the opportunity to let them go forever.

Chapter 2

The Boy

Let me begin by telling you a story about a boy. He comes from a loving family who nurtures and cares for him. His future couldn't look brighter. What this small innocent child doesn't know is that at about age 2, he will be diagnosed with severe Attention Deficit Hyperactivity Disorder (ADHD). He won't understand why he sees doctors that want to know why he does what he does, or why they give him strange tests and experiment with harsh psychotropic drugs to make him "*better.*"

At age 8, his mother will tell him about his problem and how he is not like the other children. What the boy will hear is that he is broken and that he is not and never will be "*normal.*"

This little guy does not know that by age 9 he will be sexually abused by a neighbor.

This boy will be raised in a good home, but life away from home will be torture. At age 10, while playing with friends in the bus line at school, things will get a bit too rough and out of hand. A teacher will single out this boy and grab him by the thumb, forcing it into his palm until it becomes dislocated. The more the boy cries in pain, the harder the teacher will push, smiling all the while as if enjoying the boy's suffering. In an attempt to stop the severe pain, the boy will finally punch her in the face breaking her glasses. He will become the first boy ever expelled from grade school. The teacher will never be held accountable for the injuries caused by the physical abuse.

Because of his emotional instability due to his ADHD, he will be taught never to fight, hit, etc. for any reason. He will not fight back in any way when challenged or confronted. As a result, when this boy reaches junior high, he will become the school *"pick on."* He will live in constant fear of getting beaten up at school, and the fear will be proven justified almost daily. One of the most unjust problems with being the school pick on is that YOU are always at the center of the problem. It is assumed by the authority figures at school that you are the problem. So while the bullies are sent back to class, the boy would be sent to the principal's office. In those days, corporal punishment, such as paddling with a large wooden board, was an acceptable means of behavior modification at schools. So after being beaten up by the bullies at school this boy will then be taken to the principal's office and beaten again.

Finally, the boy cannot take the beatings any longer, and at age 14 he will pull a knife at school and threaten to kill a kid if he touches him again. The kid's friends will retaliate by taking a couple of shots with hunting rifles in the general direction of the boy. The boy will go to his parents and other authority figures about the problem but will be told he is "blowing things out of proportion." Since no one will believe him, he will decide that he needs to run away for a while until things cool off. He will be gone for about three days and return at about 2 a.m. in the morning. He will go into his parent's room and tell them he is home. His mother will call the authorities, and the next morning he will be awakened by sheriff's deputies and taken to a county lockup, without the opportunity to even get dressed. He will be humiliated as he is paraded through the public courthouse without proper clothing and spend the next ten days in jail. The conditions will be bad and the poor quality and little amount of food even worse. He will lose almost ten pounds in those ten days. This event will mark the end of his emotional bond to his family for the next seven years.

At age 15 he will leave home, and by age 16 move to Los Angles California to marry his high school girlfriend. Being too young to know how to care for and treat a young wife, he will divorce by age 21.

At this point, the boy in our story has barely reached adulthood and his life has been full of trauma and pain.

What do you think will happen to this boy?

What kind of person will he become?

What are the odds he'll end up in long-term prison?

Would violence almost certainly be part of this young man's life?

Will he re-create and pass on the violent traits so prevalent in his early childhood?

Would sexual confusion and/or deviance be a real possibility?

How about his career?

Will he be able to keep gainful employment?

Will he have issues with authority?

How about anger issues?

How might the effects of anger and resentment be played out in his life?

What about relationships?

Will this young man ever be able to form healthy and trusting bonds in relationships?

What kind of father will this young man become?

Will his children be safe?

What patterns will be passed on to the next generation?

What will become of his children?

The answers to these questions are frightening. Everything we know from psychology and criminology suggests the boy is going to have major problems. With each new victimization, the odds of alcoholism, chemical abuse and addiction increase.

I attended a Victims Advocate Training Program where an expert in chemical dependency and addiction gave the odds of a person becoming addicted based on certain life circumstances. I added up all the numbers from this boy's life, and theoretically, he had a 255% chance of becoming chemically dependent. Not good odds to say the least. He is likely to be in and out of the court system for various crimes. That bright future he had when we began his story at age 2 has certainly faded away if not vanished all together.

So what did happen to this boy? Well, I can tell you from personal experience that none of those possibilities came to be in MY life. Yes, this is my story. I experienced the things in this story and many more as a child and although it was not easy, I was able to overcome them all.

With the help of a few good friends and some family members, I pulled my life together, and at age 24 met and married a wonderful woman named Janine with whom I would share a healthy, happy life. We had four beautiful children—Rachel, Matthew, Esther, and Caleb. We were as close to the perfect family as I could hope for. Sixteen amazing years passed and life had turned out great.

That's when I got the call.

Chapter 3

The Call

It was mid-afternoon on June 28th. My brother and his family had just moved from out of state to a town about an hour and a half away from our home. We had moved from the same general location they had lived the previous year. The cousins had not seen each other in that time, and we had planned to get together on a Thursday to exchange kids for a sleep over. The children were excited to be reunited with the cousins. I had some work to do at my office and was going to meet Janine and the kids at my brother's house. I wrapped things up at my desk, called my wife, and asked her to run a quick errand for me on the way, then headed out.

I was picking up a trailer for my brother when the phone rang. It was my good friend and business associate. He said, "Ben, I need you to stop whatever you're doing and listen to what I have to tell you . . .

there's been an accident. I think it's serious. I just got a call from someone who saw the advertising phone number we have on your car window. It sounds real bad. I don't know anything else."

I asked him where the accident happened, and he told me. I was five minutes ahead of them. I turned around and raced to the scene. I pulled up to a roadblock where state police had secured a perimeter. A quarter mile down the highway, a great number of emergency workers swarmed the scene. As I jumped from my truck, a Life Flight helicopter took off and accelerated over my head to the South and an ambulance sped away to the north, siren screaming.

I approached the officer at the roadblock and told him I had received a call that my family was involved in an accident. He asked me what kind of car they were driving, and I gave him a description. He paled as he told me to hold on. He got on his radio to someone up at the site and informed the person, "The father is here and wants to come up to the crash site." The response was short, grim, and terrifying, "That would NOT be advisable." As the radio transmission ended, my heart broke, lodging firmly in my throat as I realized that death had entered my life.

I asked the officer for the status of my family and was informed that someone would come and speak with me shortly. A sheriff's deputy came down from the site a few minutes later. Again I asked the status of my family. He hemmed and hawed a bit so I pressed him further. I said, "I know I have lost family up there. I can feel it. I need to know if I have anyone left, and if so, where they're being taken." After a long pause he said, "I'm sorry sir, but your wife and one of your children are dead in the car. A little boy and girl were flown to a pediatric trauma center about thirty-five miles to the south. The little girl was nonresponsive when they left. Another child has been taken by ambulance to a hospital about six miles to the north."

I knew the two little ones would be Esther and Caleb but didn't know which of my children was dead. I asked the deputy who had been taken in the ambulance. He said he did not know. I asked whether the child still in the car was a boy or a girl so that I could determine who had been taken. The deputy radioed up to the crash site and asked. The response was sterile and to the point, "Too much damage, unable to identify gender." I nearly collapsed.

I was in a daze. Time began to slow. I was losing control of my faculties. Seeing my emotional crisis and desperate need for answers, the deputy contacted the ambulance crew and determined that they had a girl and she had been slipping in and out of consciousness. I then knew my 11 year-old son, Matthew, was dead.

My friend who had called me arrived and caught me up in a hug as I told him the news through my tears.

There was no time to grieve, no time to acknowledge the loss. I had to think, make decisions of where to go first and what to do.

Since my daughter Rachel had been semiconscious, I decided to get to her as she was alone and might be aware of what was going on. My friend drove and we headed to the hospital just six miles away. We were on the wrong side of the accident and were locked in the traffic with everyone else so it took an agonizing fifty-five minutes to reach the hospital. When we arrived, Rachel had been sedated and was being wheeled out to be transferred to a level-one trauma unit by helicopter. Before I could do much of anything she was gone. Again, I was on the wrong side of the accident, and I didn't know how to get to the hospital where all my children now were. It took another two hours and fifteen minutes to reach the hospital and the remnants of my once happy family.

I arrived to the most horrific scene I have ever experienced. There, in the pediatric ICU and Emergency Center, I found three rooms. Bloody gauze, sheets, and medical implements were strewn seemingly without care. Two of the rooms were empty, and I was afraid of what that might mean. In the remaining room, I found my daughter Rachel, bruised, unconscious, and on life support. I was informed that Caleb had a very small chance of survival and that Esther was much worse off than him. Members of my extended family had arrived before I did and continued to come.

When Esther was finally brought back to her room, she was so badly disfigured that I could barely recognize her as my daughter. I could hardly bear to see her in such a condition. Over the next twenty-four hours, Esther would succumb to her injuries and die. To my great sorrow, I would not be by her side when she left this life. Rachel awoke and was asking for her mother, Caleb was going downhill fast, and medical decisions had to be made by what seemed like the hour. Organ donor choices had to be completed. I finally collapsed on a cot in a tiny closet-size room off the ICU. Laying there in the dark, I realized I didn't even know where they had taken the bodies of my wife and son. I began to tremble and shake so badly that I eventually threw up. My sister came in and sat with me until I fell asleep. She was very patient.

As Caleb deteriorated, I got a crash course in brain trauma, coma, and intercranial pressure and quickly became versed in what each of the readouts on the many machines in his room meant. On the second day, Caleb's brain pressure was high and his brain activity became virtually zero. As I sat quietly in his room with the door mostly closed, I overheard a couple of nurses talking in the hall about how sad it was that I had already lost three members of my family, and it was most likely only a matter of time before it became four. I sat there in silence crying and praying.

On July 4th, my daughter Rachel was stable enough to be released. We drove the fifty miles home together and entered the house for the first time since the accident. Coats that would never be used again hung on hooks by the door. Toys that would never be played with again lay randomly across the living room floor. A list sat on the counter of all the activities the kids could do with their cousins when they got back to the house. Dinner had been thawing in the oven waiting to be turned on. There would be no celebrating this fourth of July.

Rachel was afraid to sleep alone in the empty house and curled up next to me on her mother's side of the bed. We lay there awake listening to the pop of fireworks in the distance. I don't remember sleeping.

We waited nine days for the funeral. I didn't know if there would be another body to bury, and I couldn't go through a funeral twice in one week. Miraculously, small spikes, bumps and waves began to appear on the readouts and screens in Caleb's room. Brain activity was beginning to reappear. So, with a little faith, I moved forward with the funerals.

On July 7th, I pulled up to a chapel with three hearses parked in front. I was shocked and disturbed by the sight. We had a beautiful service and the eighteen pallbearers carried my wife and children gently to the mass open grave. With little time to grieve, we prayed, walked away from the graves, and returned to the hospital.

This tragedy was only beginning as I would be working with a traumatized daughter, grappling not only with the death of so many of her family, but also her own survival. We would spend months in hospitals and rehabilitation centers trying to recover as much of Caleb as possible.

This story does not end. I would later learn that an impaired driver had killed my family. Life would never be the same again. The trials of this accident would continue in various forms for many years to come.

I acknowledge here and now that I have no idea the suffering you have been through in your life or the exquisite agony that your own traumas and trials have caused. I didn't tell you my story to shock you, to make you feel pity, or to make you think I've had it worse. I shared it so that you would know that I've had a little experience with pain; I know a little about suffering. And . . .

. . . I have found a way out!

Chapter 4

Your Story

What kind of injuries, traumas and pains have you experienced in your life? Have you suffered abuse, violence, maybe even rape? What about verbal or emotional abuse? Have you suffered the ridicule of peers or been inappropriately judged? Have you been through a tough divorce or been betrayed by a close friend? These are just a few of the many injuries that can cause pain and suffering in our lives. Pain that becomes so much a part of us that we carry it like baggage.

We're going to go on a little journey of discovery to identify the injuries that are causing pain and suffering in your life.

We will not be reliving these experiences or the emotional pain associated with them—

—we will only be identifying them and making a list.

We cannot heal what we do not acknowledge.

At the back of this book you will find a few pages to take notes on the insights you have as you read. Take advantage of capturing your experience with notes.

Please do not skip any exercise in this book. We will be building on the insights gained from each exercise experience.

First, find a quiet place to be where you will be uninterrupted for the next fifteen to twenty minutes. Some low instrumental music in the background might be appropriate.

Now, take out your pencil and paper and make a list of all the injuries you have had in your life. You can put them in order by event, by significance, or however they come to your mind. Spend a good ten minutes or more on this so your list is as complete as you can make it. Remember, you are not stopping to feel the emotions or relive the experiences while making our lists.

Ben S. Howard

Injury List

Overcoming Life's Trauma

If you've started reading again and you're not finished with your list ... STOP! Don't cheat yourself.

The exercises in this book are important. They are a critical part of receiving the healing that is available to you. Please complete each exercise before moving on. I sincerely want you to get the most out of this experience.

Okay, now that you have your list, I'd like to take you on a little journey. Read the next section slowly. Ponder and consider each question individually.

I'd like you to imagine a meadow. You can create this meadow any way you like.

What kind of grass is in your meadow?

Is it long, short, wavy?

Are there wild flowers in your meadow?

Does your meadow have any water?

Is there a pond, lake, river or stream?

Do trees surround your meadow?

What kind of trees are they?

Are they pine, oak, pecan, aspen, or ash?

Feel the gentle breeze and allow it to bring to you the smells of your meadow.

Is it woodsy, earthy, floral, or crisp?

What sounds are present in your meadow?

Can you hear the breeze as it passes through the trees?

Are there sounds of wildlife, birds or insects in the distance?

Picture the beautiful blue sky above.

Is it clear, or are there fluffy white clouds floating through the air?

    This meadow is safe and completely protected from all danger and harm. Nothing can hurt you in your meadow.

    While your meadow forms, take a moment. Feel the quite peace that exists in this place.

As you enjoy the comfort of your meadow, you look up and notice a light, above you in the distance. It is not the sun but is very bright and completely white. As you watch, this light begins to descend slowly toward you. You are not afraid. There is something oddly comforting about this light, and as it descends, you find yourself wanting to embrace it. It continues slowly to come down until it rests gently upon your head. A warm sense of peace washes over you.

Now, I want you to allow this light to enter inside you. Allow it to come down through the top of your head. The light moves through your shoulders and out to the tips of your fingers. It continues down though your torso and into your legs until it finally reaches the very tips of your toes.

The light feels so warm and comforting that you find yourself completely relaxed. Take a moment and let the light completely fill you.

This light is very special and has the power to teach and enlighten us. With the light illuminating you from the inside, I would like you to direct your attention inside yourself. Look into the very core of your being. As you look, you will notice some dark spots or spaces that don't seem to be illuminated by this light. We are not going to touch these dark spots, and the idea of doing so is strangely uncomfortable.

As you look at one of these dark spaces, you will notice a label. This label will tell you what that dark spot is. Read the label and write it on the list you made earlier. Then return inside and find the label of the next dark spot. Do not rush this process and continue until you have written down the labels of each dark spot.

When you are done, return to your meadow. Let its peace and safety wash over you.

Then, when you're ready, come back into the awareness of your surroundings.

♡♡♡

Take a moment and look at your experience with this exercise. Were you able to experience the meadow? If you are not a visual person your meadow may be more of a story than a place. You didn't do it wrong. Your experience will be unique to you. How about the dark spots? Were the labels the same or different from your original list? There is no wrong answer here. Many times during the meadow experience, deep or even forgotten traumas that are unresolved reveal themselves. At this point, if you feel that you need to, you can repeat the exercise.

If you're like most people, you probably have a good sized list. Some items will be small but there will be some really big stuff as well. If you have a few major issues that are maintaining the center of your focus, and your list is limited to those, that's just fine. Again, this is your journey, and whatever you need to address will come out at the right time.

I grew up on a small farm in Idaho. When I was around nine years old we had a pig. We saved table scraps and other *slop* which we took out to feed the pig each day. One day I was taking some slop out to the pig. I climbed onto the fence and, balancing there with the bucket handle in one hand, I began lifting the bottom of the bucket to pour the contents into the pig's trough. As I swung the bucket, I lost my grip on the bottom and the full weight of the slop and bucket pulled me right over the fence. I landed flat on my back in the filthy, manure-filled pig pen. As I rolled over and used my hands to get up to a kneeling position, I found myself completely covered in swine crap.

If you have ever been near a pig farm, you know it was disgusting and I reeked. What do you think was the first thing I did? Did I lie back down and roll around in it? Did I scoop up handfuls of pig dung and put it in my pockets for later? Of course not! That would be completely ridiculous. And yet, isn't that exactly what we do with the injuries and traumas in our lives. We wallow in them. We pick them up and carry them with us, and they become a filthy stinking burden that steals our joy and happiness.

What did I do when I found myself covered in pig crap? I ran for the hose as fast as I could to get that nasty, filthy stink off of me.

Could ending all of the pain and suffering caused by the things on your list be as easy as running for the hose? That depends on you.

Let me ask you a simple question.

Could you be completely healed of all these traumas and injuries today?

Okay, stop shaking your head laughing. This is a serious question. In my live presentation the participants sometimes say:

"Not a chance in Hell!"

"Maybe."

"I doubt it."

"I hope so."

I think, for most people, the honest answer is, *"I don't believe it's possible."* I can understand that. For most of us, we have been carrying our baggage for a very long time. We've tried to get rid of it, sometimes through personal study, professional counseling or therapy, and still our injuries remain.

So what would it take to be completely healed of all of your injuries? The answer I usually get is, *"It would take a Miracle!"* So let me give you my own simple definition of a miracle.

Miracle:

Something impossible that happens anyway.

While you're reading this book, I am going to ask you to do something. I want you to suspend doubt for just a little while and believe that anything is possible. If you come to the end of the book and nothing happens, nothing is lost. However, while you are reading this book . . .

. . . Expect a Miracle!

Chapter 5

The Force

To do anything with our injuries we must start with some basic knowledge about the forces that affect our lives.

There are five basic forces that affect us. They are:

Physical

Emotional

Social

Psychological

Spiritual

There is a great deal of knowledge amassed about physical, emotional, social, and even the psychological forces that affect us. Doctors, psychologists, therapists, and others have written many books on these subjects. The forces that seem to most elude our understanding are the spiritual forces that surround us.

Disclaimer:
This is not a religious book.

The material we will discuss here is *Universal Truth* and cannot be claimed by any one individual denomination. That being said, let's talk a little bit about Spirit.

Philosophers, scientists, mathematicians, sages, and religious leaders, have tried to define the *Spirit* for millennia.

It's been called:

Our Subtle Self

Our Inner Being

The Watcher

The Soul

The Subconscious

The ID or I AM

Our Life Force or Energy

Let's see if we can't take a little of the mystery out of matters of the spirit. Let's take a look at our spiritual self.

Have you ever lost your temper? I mean completely lost it. Screaming, yelling, throwing plates, etc. We're talking total loss of control here. I think we're all a little embarrassed to admit that we have. I'd like you to remember a time when this happened to you, and let's see if you don't remember that experience going something like mine.

There was a time I had just completely lost control. I was ranting, raving, and totally freaking out. There came a point where it was like I was watching somebody else. Here I was completely going bananas, and way back in the back of my mind, there I was, totally calm. I remember watching myself completely out of control and, from this calm place, thinking . . .

Dude! You are losing it! Get a Grip!

Behind all the rage going on in my conscious mind, there was a part of me that stood apart. It was calm and in complete control. Do you remember that part of you when you had this experience? That is the spirit part of you. That is the part of you I want to communicate with during the remainder of this book. I don't want to talk to the conscious mind, but rather to that *Inner Being* that is the real you.

***

There are two opposing spiritual forces. We all have our own words or descriptions for these forces and they are primarily based on our own belief systems. Some examples would be:

Good vs Bad

Light vs Dark

Right vs Wrong

Yin vs Yang

God vs Devil

Christ vs Satan

Positive Energy vs Negative Energy

"Luke Sky-Walker" vs "The Dark Side"

Regardless of the words we use, we are talking about *Universal Forces* and *Universal Truth*. I come from a Christian belief system, so my words would be God or Christ and the Devil or Satan. My good friend Steve, who lives in Thailand, follows a more eastern philosophy and would use the words Yin and Yang, Good and Bad Karma or Positive and Negative Energies.

As we proceed, if the words I use to describe spiritual forces don't work for you, substitute the words that most closely fit your own belief system. *Universal Truth is Universal Truth*. It is felt at the very core of our being and we know when we hear it. We'll be checking in using our own *Inner Truth* or *Inner Light* from time to time to verify we are on the right track.

* * *

We all feel the effects of these opposing spiritual forces every day. Each of these forces works similarly. One uses truth to persuade. The other uses counterfeit to deceive. It is these counterfeit deceptions that cause a great deal of struggle in our lives.

How can we defend ourselves against these counterfeit deceptions?

*The answer can be found
in how spiritual communication works.*

Chapter 6

Spiritual Communication

To understand spiritual communications we need to start with some fundamental truths. In my personal belief system, all things light or good come from God; all things bad or dark come from the devil. Simply said, good is good, bad is bad, and they don't intermix. Good and evil are in constant and direct opposition to one another.

Let's check in with our own *Inner Truth*. Can bad be good, or can good be bad? As we look inside we know the answer. The answer can only be no.

Having this basic understanding gives us a lot of power and insight into these spiritual forces. When things happen in our lives, the associated feelings and emotions are clear indicators of whether light or dark forces are at play. Are feelings of sadness, frustration, or loneliness light or dark emotions?

Of course they're dark, and they each have their polar opposites. On the light side we have happiness, peacefulness, and love. None of these opposites can exist inside of us at the same time.

I think we have clearly established that good comes from the light side and bad comes from the dark side.

These two opposing forces operate by intelligent design. Have you ever noticed when you're really down and at your weakest point, the dark side seems to *choose* that moment to just hammer you. It sure seems that way to me.

We are continuously receiving *gifts* from one of these two sides. Good gifts are things we want in our life. They bring us more joy and peace.

Since good gifts are things we want, we're going to spend our time talking about how to rid ourselves of the dark gifts that we don't want. Dark gifts bring sadness, destruction, depression, and misery.

Why would we receive these dark gifts? Surely we can see them coming. Hence, deception has to be the greatest tool, and subtlety the delivery mechanism of the dark side. Since we would reject blatant attempts at dark influence, the dark side uses smooth and unobtrusive methods to plant negative ideas and feelings. It whispers in our ear, puts opportunities in our path, or reads and encourages our weaknesses.

How do these dark ideas and feelings enter? How does spiritual communication work? The answer is found in how our inner spirit communicates with us. Think about this. The answer is very simple.

Spiritual communication comes into our conscious mind as thought and impression. It is also often confirmed by a feeling or emotion.

Let me give you an example of a good gift, or spiritual communication, that I've had. I was driving home and had the thought, "I ought to stop and pick up some flowers for my wife." I did, and when I got home, I found that she had had an absolutely terrible day. The flowers made her feel so much better, and I got to be my sweetheart's super hero. One small spiritual communication; two really good gifts.

So was the flower idea mine? I had no idea of my wife's struggle. I suggest that the spark of the idea, the very initiating thought was not mine but a gift from God or the good side. What I did with it afterward was all me. I like to think of it as spiritual voice mail.

Likewise, I suggest that we receive negative gifts from the dark side in the same manner. That first little push didn't start within us, but what we do with it afterward is all ours. Let me give you an example.

I was driving down the freeway one day and some truck completely cut me off. I immediately got a little gift from the dark side. I got a spark of irritation laced with anger and frustration. That was the gift from the dark side. What I did with it, I'm embarrassed to say, was all me.

After those examples you might be thinking, "Wait a minute! I'm in control and making my own choices. I'm not being mind controlled. I have free will!" You are absolutely right.

Could I have chosen a different course? When that initial gift came, did I have another option? Was I free to choose a course that didn't follow the initial spark? Of course I was.

Spiritual communication never overrides free will.

What do we do when we receive a gift from the dark side we don't want?

Let's say that we are neighbors and I walk up to you on your porch and hand you a paper sack. You look inside the sack and discover it's all the dog crap that *my* dog left on *my* lawn. Is it yours just because I handed it to you? Of course not. *My dog, my crap.* So what would you do? You've got this nasty, stinky gift. What are you going to do with it?

If someone gives you something that is theirs, and you don't want it . . .

. . . Give it Back!

Chapter 7

Give it Back

Now that we know what to do with these little dark gifts, let's try an experiment. I want you to remember a negative thought or emotion that you've had in the last few days.

Warning!

This negative thought or emotion must be extremely small and not tied to anything large, ongoing, or historical. If you're in the middle of a messy divorce and your ex ticked you off, this is too big and tied to too much. Pick something simple and isolated such as an annoyance, a small offense, or something insignificant like my freeway story.

Take a moment to recall the experience. Remember the feelings and emotions you had during the event. Since I asked you to think of a negative experience, clearly these feelings and emotions will be negative in nature. They might be feelings such as anger, frustration, disappointment, annoyance, sadness, irritation, etc.

Now what if the original spark, that initiating push if you will, didn't come from you? It isn't yours. Do you want to keep it? If the answer is "yes", burn this book now! You have no further use of it. If the answer is "no", read on.

Since you're still reading, I presume you don't want to keep this dark gift that isn't yours. So let's see if we can't get rid of it.

We are going to do a little exercise. Are you ready?

I want you to repeat after me in your mind:

> *"Until this moment, I didn't realize that that negative thought or emotion wasn't mine. I thought it was just my response to the situation or problem. Now that I know that it isn't mine, I don't want to keep it."*

Now I want you to allow that negative thought or emotion to go back out of you the same way it came in. Simply release it back out by the same path it entered.

Were you successful? How long did that take? The typical time in my live presentation is two to four seconds. If you had trouble with this, you picked something too big. Pick something smaller and try again.

Having had success, how does it feel? What emotion and or feeling did you feel when that little piece of darkness was let go? Think about the feelings that came.

Some typical feelings might be:

Relief

Peace

Calm

Lighter

Happiness

Joy

Quiet

Think about what your feelings and emotions were. It may be one or more of these or may be unique to you, but it will be one thing for sure—good!

Let's examine what happened here. You took something dark and negative, something that was initiated from the dark side, and released it back to where it came from. What immediately followed? You gave back your dark gift and immediately received a light gift or a good gift. Did you ask for it? Did you expect it? You didn't. It just happened. Think about that for a moment.

Now, look at your watch. At this time, on this day, you had a little miracle. God interacted personally, directly, and spiritually with you. Again, don't get caught up on my words. Use the words of your belief system.

Universal Truth is Universal Truth.

Chapter 8

Justification

What are some reasons we don't give back our negative experiences? Why do we sometimes hold on to the pain and trauma in life? It seems to make no sense that we would hang on to the burden of pain, hate, anger, abuse, victimization, etc. Here are a few of those reasons and there are many more.

We want to.

"I have been hurt and nobody has the right to tell me everything is okay."

We think it does something for us.

"I'm hurt, so people treat me differently."

We think it protects us.

"Since I'm already hurt and living in pain, I won't feel the effect of the new pain."

We feel justified in our feelings or positions.

"How they hurt me was wrong, and I have a right to be angry and punish them."

It keeps us from having to put forth effort to change.

"It's not my fault; they're the ones who hurt me. I can't fix it."

It allows us to avoid working at being better or accountable.

"I'm a rape and abuse victim. You can't expect *that* from me."

It allows us to justify our addictions and/or inappropriate behaviors.

"Because my father was an alcoholic, I'm an alcoholic. I'm this way because I was abused."

Justifications like these are one of the biggest hurdles to letting the pain and suffering in our lives go. We can't let something go that we're using or justifying. Let me tell you a story that may illustrate this point.

There was a man that married a woman who had several teenage and young adult children. The mom was excited to share the joy of her new relationship with her children, and the man was very excited about the opportunity to have more children in his life. The children were used to a certain type of home environment. For older teens and young adults, change is not always a welcome thing. Friends, life patterns, and schools were all centered on life with mom as a single parent. Marriage meant moving, changing schools, making new friends; all very difficult changes. Their feelings of fear and frustration are absolutely valid.

The children now have a choice in their lives. They can adapt to change and embrace the opportunity to build a new and maybe better life, or reject change and attempt to justify their position. Again we see the clear separation of light and dark. One leads to family unity, happiness and peace. The other leads to contention, disaccord and war.

Unfortunately for this couple, the children elected the second of these two choices. The children decided the marriage was a bad thing for them and they didn't want it. From this point forward, they began the task of justifying and/or validating their position.

To justify their position in rejecting their mother's new marriage and their failure to participate in the new family, they were forced to create problems or demonize the man and the relationship. When mom moved in with her new husband, the children refused to come and blamed the man for destroying their family and tearing their family apart. Was this true? No; in fact, just the opposite. Every attempt was being made to bring the family closer together. To counter that complaint, opportunities to play, share time and have fun were created.

The claim of breaking up the family having been invalidated, a new problem had to be created to continue to justify their position. Enter: *The Blame Game*. The new tactic for justification was, "All our problems are his fault. If he just did this or that, etc." Not having success with the blame game, they moved on to finding fault and spreading it through the extended family to build support for the position they were trying to justify. The man would attempt to clear up the false statements and misrepresentations and immediately upon achieving a resolution another would be created.

Do you see a vicious cycle here? As long as the

children are intent on justifying their position, every time one justification is resolved, another will be created in an endless cycle of misery.

The saddest thing about justification is that we are virtually always justifying our own self-deceptions.

Clearly justification is not our friend and does not help us. It does nothing but prevent us from having what we really want.

How many of our injuries and traumas are we using this powerfully negative tool to hold on to?

If you're using it, you can't let it go.

Look at the injuries and traumas on your list. Take a moment and think about each one and ask yourself this question. "Am I using it?"

Are you using it to justify anger? Are you using it to rationalize or validate a thought or position? Are you using it to justify inappropriate actions or behaviors? Be honest with yourself here. No one is looking over your shoulder. Put the letter "J" by each item that you are using. Remember,

If you're using it, you're keeping it.

If you're using it, you're keeping it along with all of its pain and emotion.

Now go back and look at all of those items you marked. Think about how much suffering they've caused you and continue to cause in your life. Are you willing to quit using it to be free? Again, be honest with yourself. If you're not ready to stop using something, you can't let it go, and guess what?

That's okay!

Accept it. Embrace it. Own it. Own the fact that this injury is yours and you're hanging on to it. *There's great power in this because if you own it, you control it, and its destiny is yours to decide.*

At this point, if you're willing to stop using an item that you've marked with a "J", remove that mark.

Now that you've decided what pain and suffering you want to keep in your life . . .

. . . let's move on and talk about eliminating those items that you don't want.

Chapter 9

Pain

There are two types of pain that we experience in life. The pain from the actual experience and the pain we carry forward through life after the experience.

There is nothing we can do about the pain from the actual experience. We're going to go through it. When my family was killed, I could not stop the pain that was coming. There was absolutely no way to avoid it. Pain and suffering are part of life. They help us grow and become better, stronger, and wiser. I am a better person because of the things that I've been through. I rarely judge others; I can meet people *where they're at*. I've received a profound understanding of the depth of human sorrow and have developed deep compassion. I've received many other gifts from these difficult lessons in my life. So there can be an upside to negative and traumatic experiences.

Caution!
We cannot receive the benefit or upside from our trials until we're through with them.

Still want to justify hanging onto your stuff? It may be time to rethink that.

If you're continue to carry the pain and trauma associated with the experience, you're not through with it. So how do we finish? How do we end the pain and suffering from a trauma or injury when the experience has passed? How do we avoid carrying that pain forward? There is a very simple and *Universal Truth* that is the answer to this question.

Unfortunately the answer has been propagated with misunderstandings and misconceptions that prevent us from using it. Most of us have tried but the lack of clear truth and understanding on this subject keeps us in pain and unable to use it.

The Big Reveal

The title of this book could really be *The Healing Power of Forgiveness*. Why isn't that the title of this book? Because, chances are, you wouldn't have picked it up!

The first thing that most people think of when we talk about forgiveness is, "I can't do it," It doesn't work," or "The offender doesn't deserve it." Based on most of our past experiences and knowledge, all of these things would be true. Let's address some of the reasons we don't forgive.

The reason most of us don't forgive is that we have some fundamental misconceptions about what forgiveness is and is not. Many of these misconceptions are learned at a very young age in family, school, or church. The words used to describe forgiveness do not always communicate the *Universal Truth* of the matter. For example, most of us believe that forgiveness requires the following three things:

1. *Embrace the offender.*

We feel that if we forgive, we have to embrace the offender and let them back in. How many times have we heard *"Forgive and Forget."* We think somehow true forgiveness means we have to *forget about it* and allow them back into our lives.

2. *What they did was okay.*

It feels like if we forgive them, what we're really saying is that what they did was okay. This sounds ridiculous, but we can see it in the very words we use. Let's say Mary did something really offensive. She comes back to you a couple days later and says, "Gee, I'm really sorry about that." How will you respond? You'll probably respond like most, "Oh, it's okay."

It's not okay! It will never be okay! Our very language perpetuates this critical misconception of forgiveness. I can't bear this terminology. If someone apologizes to me I don't say, "It's okay," because it wasn't. I simply say, "Thank you, I appreciate that," or "That means a lot to me." I never say, "It's okay." That just feels wrong to my own personal *Inner Truth*. How about yours?

3. *We fear that we'll be letting them get away with it.*

It feels like if we forgive the offender we are letting them get away with what they did to us. For Christians, it feels like if we forgive them, so will Jesus and the person will no longer be accountable for their actions. Again, something in my *Inner Truth* says this is wrong.

None of these things are part of true forgiveness.

Just in case I wasn't clear, let me repeat.

None of these things are required by forgiveness.

Let's do a quick check in with our own *Inner Truth*. If we don't have to let someone back in who's hurt us, and forgiveness does not make what they did okay, and it doesn't let them get away with it, are we more open to the idea of forgiveness?

I want to say right now, that if you haven't been able to let go of the big stuff in your life there is a reason.

It's not your fault.

There is *Universal Law* at play here. You cannot accomplish forgiveness outside the natural affect of *Universal Law*.

So, let's take a look at the requirements of Universal Law.

Chapter 10

Universal Law

What does *Universal Law* require for us to let something go? When someone has done something to hurt us, what do we need to release it? We need something. We can feel it. What is it? Let's check in with our *Inner Truth*. When someone has done something terrible to us, what do we need to let it go?

We need an apology.

We need the offender to acknowledge what they have done, to acknowledge that they have hurt us, and to humbly repent to us and make recompense to make it right.

Or we need justice.

We need for the offender to be forced to make just recompense for the injuries they have caused. We need to know that they have paid an appropriate price for their actions.

Let's talk about each of these two core needs.

Apology

When we've been hurt by someone, a true apology, or put another way, humble repentance to us, can often give us the ability to *grant* mercy. I don't mean someone saying a half hearted, "I'm sorry." That just makes me think, "You're sorry all right, you lousy #$%&@!" I mean a humble, sincere, heart-felt apology with a true willingness to make it right.

I had a partner in business to whom I had loaned quite a sum of money to help him grow his business. Over time, he made a number of inappropriate choices outside of our agreement on how he used the money. Consequently, he lost it all. I was very disappointed that he had broken the agreement and acted without authority. He had committed a serious offense. I was very hurt and needed *Universal Law* to be satisfied to let it go.

So what happened? This man did not go into hiding and stop taking my calls. He came to me and, in tears, admitted what he had done. He apologized with great fervency and promised he would do everything in his power to repay his debt. He asked me to forgive him, fully expecting that I would not.

What would you do? Here was a man asking forgiveness and mercy from me, willing to accept the consequences of his actions and make it right. This man was following the requirements of *Universal Law,* and when I looked inside, at my own *Inner Truth*, I found that I was no longer injured and angry. I no longer felt the need for justice. I was left with nothing but compassion.

The injury in this story was completely resolved with the apology side of *Universal Law*.

Can we expect the offenders in our lives to do what this man did? Probably not. How many offenders use this option? Almost none. This leaves us with the second option we have to settle and let go of our traumas and injuries.

Justice

Lacking a true apology, when we have been hurt by an offender, we have a core need for justice. My friend Debbie sits in courtrooms every day as part of her job. She sees the pain and suffering caused by the acts of violent criminals, drunk and impaired drivers, drug addicts, etc. She sees their victims come into the court, day after day, seeking justice for the crimes and offenses which were committed against them.

Why do these victims plead for maximum sentences, fierce punishments, and more? It is because they know that the offender is not going to apologize, repent, or make things right with them. Because of this, they feel that true justice is the only thing they can hope for to find peace and relief. So how many find *real* peace and relief from the justice laid out by courts of law? Very few. They rarely feel that they have received true justice. It usually feels hollow and empty. *Inner Truth* never seems to say to them, "It is done. It's settled. I'm satisfied." The long awaited peace does not come with the sentencing of the offender.

Justice or an apology; will anything else do? What does your *Inner Truth* tell you?

If someone has intentionally injured us, our *Inner Truth* tells us we must have one of these two things. This is called the *Universal Law of Justice and Mercy*. We cannot let something go without dealing with this *Universal Law*. We can stick it on a shelf, we can ignore it and *pretend* we let it go; we can *therapy* it, but in the end, when we get hurt again, it comes back to the surface.

Without obtaining a true apology or true justice, it is impossible to release the pain and trauma of our injuries because the situation has not been settled. *Universal Law* has not been satisfied. Our *Inner Truth* tells us this is true.

Therein lies the rub. If *Universal Law* cannot be satisfied, we cannot let something go no matter how hard we try. So again, if you haven't gotten over the traumas and injuries of life,

It's not your fault and . . .
. . . there is a solution.

The first part of that solution is found in understanding the injuries themselves.

So, let's take a closer look at the nature of injury.

Chapter 11

The Nature of Injury

We have discussed in detail *Spiritual Forces* and *Universal Law*. It is critical to understand that what the world would call *emotional* injuries, actually begin much deeper. As we have already discovered together in the *Give It Back* exercise, our emotions and thinking patterns are directly affected by things happening at the spiritual level, i.e. by the spiritual gifts we receive.

As we look at the nature of injury, I would like to begin with an example of physical injury.

I once came upon a motorcycle accident. The cyclist had broken bones that had torn through the muscle and flesh and protruded grotesquely. He was taken to the emergency room and sent for immediate surgery.

What did the doctors fix first? Did they first start by stitching him up? Would he heal properly from this technique? Of course not. First the doctor had to repair the bone because it is the foundation and framework that the muscles and skin rely on to maintain form. Second, muscle, tendons and tissues were repaired because without them there would be no function. Third, the outer flesh was carefully sutured to minimize scaring, the outward sign of the injury.

Like physical injuries, the injuries caused by acts of sin, crime, or offense are just as real. They also exist on multiple levels and must be addressed in proper order.

Consider the following comparison.

Bone = Spirit

Muscle = Emotions and Thought Patterns

Skin = Outward Actions and Responses

Let's make a comparison using the example of the motorcyclist's physical injury to the injuries sustained by an act of sin, crime, or offense.

Let's say a spouse betrays their marriage covenant and has an affair or abandons the marriage without cause. By violating *Universal Law* through an act of sin or offense, this person has caused a substantial and very real injury. They have entered into a *debt* or *contract* that must be settled according to that same *Universal Law*.

This injury occurs at the spiritual level and is represented by the breaking of the bone in our physical example. Like the bone tearing through the muscle, this spiritual injury tears through our emotions, altering our thoughts, beliefs, and perspectives. Finally, like the bone and muscle protruding through the skin, the affects of the injury manifest in our outward actions and attitudes.

Unlike the doctor, when dealing with the injuries and traumas of life, we almost always try to fix everything backwards.

When and if we realize we are acting out because of our injury, we first try to control our actions. How effective is this? Some very strong people can alter their behaviors but most of us can only maintain control for short periods of time. Like stitching up the skin first to hide an injury, we are still dealing with the spiritual and emotional effects that have not been repaired, i.e., the broken bone and torn muscles.

Eventually we figure out, or someone else says, "*You need help!*"

Therapy, here we come! So off we go to the therapist and talk about the problem ... and talk ... and talk ... and talk. Now, we are trying to heal a spiritual injury (the bone) at the emotional or thinking level (the muscle).

Like the physical injury, the traumas and injuries that cause so much emotional torment and pain must be addressed from the inside out and in proper order.

Spirit = Bone

Emotions and Thought Patterns = Muscle

Outward Actions and Responses = Skin

First we heal the spirit self using *Universal Law* and *Universal Truth*. Many times healing at this level allows the other levels to heal naturally on their own, however, if patterns of emotion and *stinking thinking* still exist, we move on to the second level of healing.

Second, we work on healing the *stinking thinking* and defective thought patterns along with their emotional reactions. These patterns develop over time when the spiritual injury goes unaddressed. This is where therapy can make a huge difference. A good therapist can help us gain tools to restructure our thinking and regulate inappropriate emotional responses.

When this is complete, it is rare that we need to address our outward actions directly because they tend to resolve on their own, or with only a limited effort on our part.

Now with an understanding of the nature of injury . . .

*. . . let's take a look at
the five categories of injuries we face in life.*

Chapter 12

Categories

Get ready for the shortest, easiest chapter in this book.

There are five categories of injuries.

Vicarious

Incidental

Unintentional

Intentional

Ongoing and Future

Vicarious Injuries are injuries to others whom we care about that we take on personally.

Incidental Injuries are injuries to us when the offender had no idea they had hurt us, but if they realized would do anything to make it right or take it back.

Unintentional Injuries are injuries when the offender did not know better, or did not understand the gravity or pain caused by their actions. There was no intent to hurt us.

Intentional Injuries are injuries when the offender knew what they were doing, knew it was wrong and would hurt us, but did it anyway.

Ongoing and Future Injuries are injuries that will continue in our life due to circumstances beyond our control, whether the offender realizes it or not. Our worst repeat offender is sometimes ourselves. Future or new injuries that will happen to us fall into this category.

Let's take a look at each of these categories in more detail.

Chapter 13

Vicarious Injuries

Vicarious injuries are injuries to others whom we care about that we take on personally. Who do you think are the number one vicarious injury people in the world? *You have to be at least as smart as a fifth grader to get this one.* Who are they? Mothers! Why do you think mothers are the number one vicariously injured people? Because they love their kids. You mess with a mom's kids, you mess with the mom. Try messing with a bear cub and you will learn this natural law in a hurry!

Let's say little Ethan gets picked on at school. What does mom do? She immediately takes it on as her own. She rushes right down to the school and demands that little Joey, who picked on her child, be beaten to death or at least buried in a mound of ants until his bones are picked clean. Needless to say, mom is a little emotional about this. When Ethan was hurt, mom became hurt as if she'd been hurt herself. She had the same emotional response and feelings as if the injury was her own.

This is a big problem for parents today. What is the result of mom taking on this vicarious injury? Perhaps overprotection, and the enabling of a future generation. When we take on someone else's injury as our own, we tell them that we don't think they can handle it. They're not strong enough. We don't believe in them. Funny how operating from vicarious injury does exactly the opposite of what we're trying to do. Instead of becoming empowered to stand up for themselves, they become victims for life.

Why did the mom in our story do this? Why do we take on vicarious injuries? Because we love the person who's been injured. We want to help. All we want to do is take away the suffering of our loved one. I'm going to share another story about this, but before I do, it's appropriate that we go back and take another look at the two opposing forces of Good vs. Evil. One uses truth to persuade; the other uses counterfeit to deceive. Let's look at one of these counterfeits.

Sympathy vs Empathy

Let me start with the definitions of *Sympathy* and *Empathy*.

Sympathy: a) the act or capacity of entering into or sharing the feelings or interest of another, b) the feeling or mental state caused by such sensitivity.

Empathy: the action of understanding, being aware of, being sensitive to the feelings, thoughts and experience of another without having the feelings, thoughts and experience fully within oneself.

These two definitions are nearly the same and modern culture and usage would have us believe they are interchangeable. They are not. Although the difference is small, it is profound in effect. As *specifically* related to trauma, *Empathy* comes from the good side, and *Sympathy* is its counterfeit. Let's take a look at these two principles in action.

Let's say I have a close friend who falls victim to physical or sexual abuse. We'll call her Jane. I'm very close to Jane and I love her dearly as a friend. Because of this love, I am deeply affected by her trauma. All I want is for Jane to feel better. I want to support her in love and help her overcome this horrible event. If I act in sympathy, I take on Jane's injury myself and naturally take on her pain and anguish also.

Acting in sympathy from a place of injury, my *"loving"* support of Jane might look something like this.

"I can't believe this happened to you! This is the most terrible thing! How dare anyone violate you in such a way. We need to make them pay! You are so justified in feeling so hurt and angry. What a jerk! I don't blame you at all for being so sad and depressed. I am too. This whole situation demands justice."

Operating from sympathy and a place of vicarious injury, what am I doing to Jane? Am I helping her? Am I making her feel better? *I am not!* I've entered into her pain and now I am acting as a mirror, reflecting it back at her continually. While trying to love her, I am injuring her again and again, creating deep roots of pain, suffering and trauma. Is this what I wanted to do to my friend Jane? Clearly this would not be my intent.

What if I didn't take on Jane's injury? What if I acted out of empathy, acknowledging and understanding her pain and suffering, without taking it on personally. Would my response be different? Of course it would. I would be able to maintain a more independent and supportive role. Let's take a look at the same situation and how it might play out in empathy.

"I am so sorry that happened to you Jane. You know how much I love you. Nothing will ever change that. I'm here for you no matter what. Tell me how you're feeling? You are not alone."

That response had a profoundly different feel didn't it? Instead of reflecting back Jane's pain and suffering, she was allowed to release it by or through us. We didn't take it. It passed right by us, but it gave Jane the opportunity to vent her pain and receive genuine concern and relief.

In *sympathy*, can we ever fix someone else's problem? Of course not, but, in *empathy*, we can allow them to use *us* as part of *their* solution.

Let's go back to the definition of vicarious injuries. These are injuries to others whom we care about that we take on personally. By very definition are these *our* injuries? No, it's not our injury. We've chosen to take it on ourselves, but it is not ours. Was mom hurt when Ethan was hurt? No, only Ethan was hurt. Was I abused when Jane was abused? No, only Jane was abused. From these simple stories we can see that by taking on vicarious injuries we only hurt ourselves and the ones we love.

Stop it!

Time to check our *Inner Truth*. In order to let go of the vicarious injuries in our lives do *WE* need justice or an apology? Look inside yourself and find the answer to that question. When I look inside myself, the answer is no because *I* have no injury. The injury was never mine! Satisfying *Universal Law* does not apply to me for someone else's injury.

Chapter 14

Incidental Injuries

Incidental Injuries are injuries to us when the offender had no idea they had hurt us, but if they realized, would do anything to make it right or take it back. By very definition, these are injuries incidental to living.

I'd like to tell you a story about the perfect family. The perfect guy meets the perfect girl, and of course, the relationship is absolutely perfect. They decide to get married, and as all perfect couples do, before long, they have the perfect baby. This baby is completely innocent.

Overcoming Life's Trauma

There are no wounds, pains, or hurts on his little heart. Mom is the perfect mom and tends to all the baby's needs. When the baby cries, mom comes and cares; when the baby needs a diaper, mom changes it; when the baby needs food, mom feeds the baby. On one particular day things are really hectic for mom. The dinner is burning on the stove, the phone is ringing, someone is knocking at the door, and at that moment, the baby starts to cry. Mom can't come straight to the bedside. For the first time mom doesn't come.

Here we have the first tiny wound to that innocent little heart. Mom didn't come. *Doesn't she love me?* The baby has its first sense of abandonment. Time goes by and mom and dad call this child into the living room with great news. He's going to have a special friend. Mom and dad seem very excited about it. They start telling him about how his special friend will arrive soon. And then, one day, without warning, mom is gone.

Overcoming Life's Trauma

Where did she go? Will she ever come home? Another wound on that little heart. Finally, after three days, mom comes back and she has the special little friend with her. The child is so excited. He runs over, grabs the special friend by the ears and starts to pick it up. Immediately mom screams, "Don't touch the baby!" *But you said it's my special friend. Why can't I play with it? I've waited so long."* Another little wound scars the heart of the child.

Ben S. Howard

As life continues, wound after little wound begin to cover the heart, creating scars of pain and injury.

Now, do you think that if that perfect mother knew that the child had received an injury the day she didn't get there soon enough that she wouldn't do everything she could to take that injury away? Of course she would. How many injuries in life have we taken on that have been completely incidental to living? No intent to hurt us ever existed. It was simply our own perception of what had happened. The injury and the associated pain were real but an actual event to hurt us never happened. It was *perceived* only.

Look inside yourself. If you were the grown child, having had that first injury, would you need mom to come back and fix it? Now that you understand it was perceived only, do you need Justice or an Apology for this injury? Of course you don't. So it is with all incidental injuries.

Chapter 15

Unintentional Injuries

Unintentional injuries are injuries when the offender did not know better or did not understand the gravity or pain caused by their action. They had no intention to hurt us. This doesn't mean that the offender did not do something wrong. In fact, it may have been downright terrible, and yes, it caused pain. But their intent to do harm was not there. Self-inflicted injuries nearly always fall into this category as we rarely intend to hurt ourselves.

I'd like to tell you a story about a hundred things. Let's suppose there are a hundred things we need to learn in our lifetime. If we knew these hundred things we would have everything we needed. It's probably more like a million, but for the sake of our story, we'll keep it at a hundred. Let's suppose I know numbers one through ten and you know numbers eleven through one hundred. Good job, by the way.

Overcoming Life's Trauma

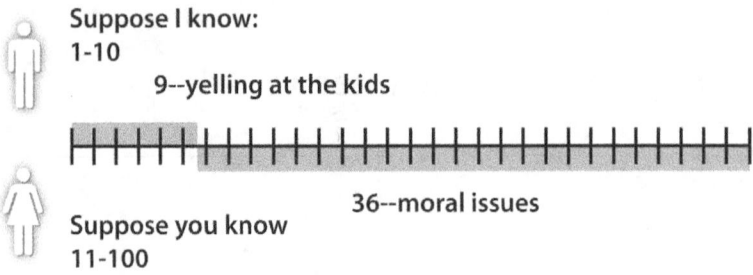

I know number nine is "don't yell at the kids." I see you at the grocery store chewing out your seven-year-old for knocking something off the shelf, calling him stupid for not keeping his hands to himself, and I think, "What a horrible person. They're definitely going straight to hell."

In the meantime, I don't know number thirty-six. Number thirty-six is morality. So while I'm sleeping with the neighbor's wife, I'm judging you for yelling at the kids.

Do you see a huge inequity here? It seems a little ridiculous that someone didn't know these two things, but what if you grew up in a family where yelling was the norm. Maybe that really was your family.

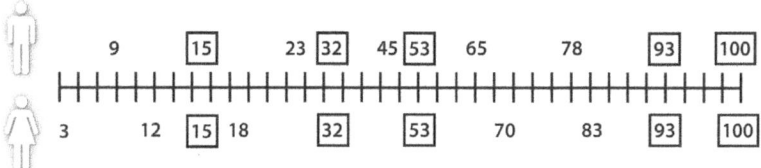

I think it's more like this. You know number three, I know number nine, you know number twelve, and we both know number fifteen. I know twenty-three, forty-five, sixty-five; you know eighteen, seventy, and eighty-three. We both know thirty-two, fifty-three, and one hundred. Based on this, there are some things that we understand together and would agree on. These are rules that we would both follow, and there would be little or no conflict. There are some things, however, that I know that you don't know. Would it be fair for me to be angry and hold you accountable for making a mistake that you had no way of knowing you made?

I recently had a gathering at my home. I had a number of guests and there were several that I did not personally know. As we sat around the table talking, this one fellow, I'll call him Grant, kept interrupting others and making offensive and inappropriate comments.

I could hardly believe that Grant did not recognize how offended and hurt some of the people at the table were becoming. Grant, however, was completely oblivious. He had no idea that the things he was doing and saying were hurting others.

Could I have taken offense to what Grant was doing? Sure, I could have. Could I have gotten in Grant's face, told him he was an idiot and to shut his trap? I could have done that too, but Grant wouldn't have had a clue what I was talking about. He would have perceived it only as a personal attack on him.

Let's check in with our *Inner Truth*. Grant made a mistake. He did something wrong, but there was no intent to hurt anyone. Do we need justice? Does Grant need to pay? It might be nice if he did, but does *Universal Law* require it? Do we need justice?

Do we need an apology? Did Grant owe the people at the table an apology? Probably, but he wouldn't even know what to apologize for. Again, when I look at my own *Inner Truth*, I find that I don't need Grant to apologize to let this go. I know that he just didn't get it, and I don't feel the need to hold him accountable for something he doesn't understand. How about you?

I find it fascinating that without the offender knowingly committing an act of sin or offense, *Universal Law* does not require the same justice or recompense which are required by intentional acts. We are free to forgive these offenses at will, if we so desire.

In the live presentation, I sometimes have participants who struggle with the principles covered in the first part of this chapter. We spend a little time discussing specific questions until we reach clarity as a group. As this isn't possible with the book, if you are struggling with the principles just discussed, then re-classify any unintentional injuries you may have, and make them intentional injuries. We will deal with them when we come to that chapter.

Let's address self-inflicted unintentional injuries.

What kind of things do we feel guilty about? Crime, sin, and offense are obvious, but what other things for which we carry guilt? Here are a few of the responses I have heard.

"I don't spend enough time with my kids."

"I'm not patient enough."

"I don't exercise enough."

"I don't have enough discipline with money."

"I don't give my husband enough attention."

"I don't go to church enough."

"I don't volunteer in the community enough."

"I can't finish enough of my wife's to-do list."

"I don't make enough money for my family."

"I can't do enough to make a difference."

"I'm just not good enough."

All this guilt that we carry brings us down, makes us feel unworthy and miserable. So this begs the question, "Is guilt good or bad?" Guilt can be a fairly difficult and uncomfortable experience.

I regularly give an hour-and-a-half presentation entitled *"Guilt Free Living."* Most often, the participant vote would come in at nearly one hundred percent that guilt is a bad thing. It certainly doesn't feel very good. It really shakes them up when I pull the "bait and switch" and tell them guilt is good.

"Hey! We showed up to become guilt free!" they cry.

Guilt is good because it is a motivator. It pushes us and drives us to change. It helps us have the desire to improve and become better. Let me give you my definition of guilt.

Guilt: The feelings or emotions caused by an act of sin, crime, or offense.

Are any of the items in the list above an act of sin, crime, or offense? None that I can see. So what is this dark feeling, if not guilt? What is this feeling that brings us down and makes us feel not good enough or like we can never be our best self? If guilt is good then there must certainly be a counterfeit opposite. That opposite is *shame*.

Shame is from the dark side. Shame does not motivate. It does not push us to do better, but leaves us in apathy. It steals our self-worth and makes us feel like we can never do any better.

Carrying the pain of shame is the most common self-inflicted injury there is. It is one of the most hurtful forms of self-abuse. I think I may have said this before.

Stop it!

Take another look at the list of items above. They're full of things that we're not doing *enough* of.

What if we said, *"Enough with enough."*

How would that feel? How freeing would that be?

Now let's go back to our story of a hundred things. How many of those things did you know when you were sixteen? I know a fifteen-year-old who reminded me that he knew *"everything!"* I guess I forgot a lot since I was fifteen. Seriously though, how many did we really know at fifteen? Four, maybe five? Then at age 30, how many more? Ten or twenty?

By age 45, I hope we at least know about half of them since we're about halfway dead.

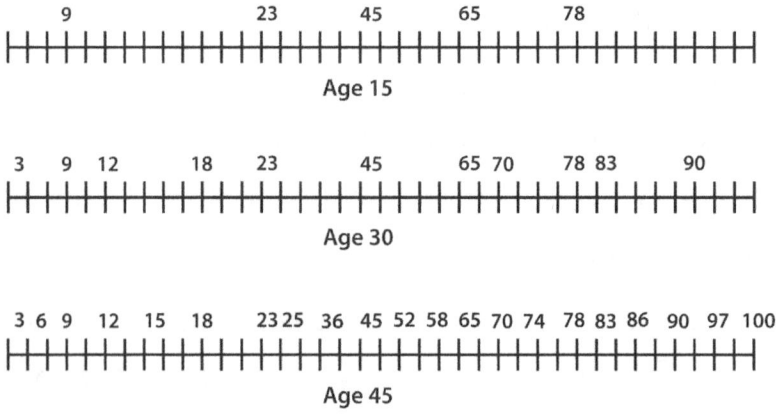

I find it odd that at age 45 we look back on ourselves at age 30 and judge ourselves for all the things that we did wrong. We say to ourselves, "I was a terrible person. I never did anything right. I'm not good enough," and so on. We would like to think if we could just do it over that we would do things differently.

The truth is, we knew what we knew, and would most likely make the same mistakes again.

Depending on our own belief system, some mistakes that we've made may require resolution through making them right, and/or working through repentance with spiritual leaders. That being said, I use a fairly simple philosophy for myself.

I'm good enough for today!

I just can't be here tomorrow.

I'm okay today. I've done my best and that's all I can hope for. Tomorrow is another day, and tomorrow, I'll do just a little better.

Again, let's check in with our own *Inner Truth*. Do you need to apologize to yourself for your shortcomings and imperfections? Do you need to punish yourself? Stop nodding your head, smarty-pants. As we look inside, we know *Universal Law* does not require it.

Chapter 16

The Meadow

We've taken a look at the first three categories of injuries. They are

Vicarious

Incidental

Unintentional

There is a common thread among each of these injuries. What is it?

Hint: What do we need to let them go?

In the Vicarious Injury chapter we learned that vicarious injuries are not, and never were, ours. They never belonged to us but we took them upon ourselves out of love for another person. What do we need to let vicarious injuries go?

In the Incidental Injuries chapter we learned that we take on injuries because of our own mistaken perception of what happened. No actual act of real offense occurred. The offense was merely perceived. What do we need to let incidental injuries go?

In the Unintentional Injuries chapter we learned that acts of offense, without intent, do not seem to require the same justice as intentional acts. We are free to forgive or grant mercy if we choose to do so. Although possibly appreciated, an apology is not mandatory for us to forgive. What do we need to let unintentional injuries go?

The answer to all these questions is the same. Have you figured it out?

[*Insert the "Jeopardy" theme song here.*]

The answer? Nothing!

We need nothing to let these first three categories of injuries go. We can simply choose to. We are free to let them go at will without having to first address the requirements of *Universal Law*.

In a moment, we're going to look at your list of injuries and put a check mark by each injury that falls into one of these first three categories. First, though, a word of caution. Since you are a considerate person, you would like to give some of the offenders in your life the benefit of the doubt and classify the injury they caused as unintentional.

Do not do this!

As you review your list, look at your own *Inner Truth*. If you have the slightest sense that you need justice or an apology for an item, it should be classified as an intentional injury and it will be addressed later in this book.

Go now to your list and mark any items that are vicarious, incidental or unintentional injuries.

Now that you have identified these items on your list, I have a very simple question. Do you want to keep them? Do you want to keep them along with their associated trauma and pain? Yes or no? I hope you answered, "No."

Remember, as we discussed in the chapter on justification, if you're *using* it, you're keeping it. Are you *using* any of these items? If you are, are you willing to stop? If you're willing to stop, let's move on.

Now that you're ready to be free of these first three categories of injuries, I'd like to take you on a little journey we've been on once before. I want you to remember your meadow. Remember it exactly how you created it.

What kind of grass is in your meadow?

Is it long, short, wavy?

Are there wild flowers in your meadow?

Does your meadow have any water?

Is there a pond, lake, river or stream?

Do trees surround your meadow?

What kind of trees are they?

If so, are they pine, oak, pecan, aspen, or ash?

Feel the gentle breeze and allow it to bring to you the smells of your meadow.

Is it woodsy, earthy, floral, or crisp?

What sounds are present in your meadow?

Can you hear the breeze as it passes through the trees?

Are there sounds of wildlife, birds or insects in the distance?

Picture the beautiful blue sky above.

Is it clear, or are there fluffy white clouds floating through the air?

This meadow is safe and completely protected from all danger and harm. Nothing can hurt you in your meadow.

While your meadow again forms, take a moment. Feel the quite peace that exists in this place.

As you enjoy the comfort of your meadow, again you look up and notice the light above you in the distance.

Again, the light begins to slowly descend toward you until it rests directly on you head. The warm familiar sense of peace washes over you.

Allow the light to enter inside you through the top of your head. The light moves through your shoulders and out to the tips of your fingers. It continues down though your torso and into your legs until it finally reaches the very tips of your toes.

Take a moment and let the light completely fill you. The light feels so warm and comforting that you find yourself completely relaxed.

Now I want you to imagine gathering up all the vicarious, incidental, and unintentional injuries in your life. Gather them up in your hands. Now, I'd like you to imagine compressing these injures down between your hands. Compress them down until they reach the size of a large grapefruit. Continue compressing as this ball of injuries passes through the size of a baseball, then a golf ball. You continue compressing by rolling the ball in your hands like cookie dough until it passes the size of a grape and finally becomes the size of a pea. Now, imagine holding your compressed injuries out in front of you in your hands.

Allow the pea size ball of injuries to slowly lift away from your hands. Let it rise into the light and as it moves away, feel the burdens and pain lifting away with it. Watch the pea move up into the light and begin to fade away in the distance. When it is completely gone, become aware again of your meadow. Let the peace and safety of your meadow wash over you. Take a moment to feel the peace and freedom from your injuries.

Then, when you're ready, come back to the awareness of your surroundings.

What happened? What feelings did you experience? Like the simple *Give it Back* process we experienced earlier, what happened when we let the negative or dark experiences in our life go? Did you feel the positive energy, feelings, or spirit come to you? If the answer is yes, I want you to pause and give thanks or gratitude in your own way because, by my definition, *you just received another miracle!*

Go back to your list. Cross out all the checked items that no longer hold pain or negative emotion. The rest will be dealt with later.

You might be thinking, "That was easy because none of these were *real* injuries! None of it was the big stuff.

Well, on to the Big Stuff!

Chapter 17

Intentional Injuries

You have been very patient. I acknowledge that here we are in chapter seventeen and we still haven't addressed any of our big, traumatic and painful injuries. These are the things that cause the true agony and sorrow of life. I've already shared my story, and you've learned that I know a little bit about pain and suffering.

I want to reiterate again, if you haven't been able to let go of the big stuff...

...it's not your fault.

There is *Universal Law* at play here. So let's quickly recap *Universal Law*.

Let's review the three reasons we can't forgive. Do you remember what they are?

Justification

Justice

Apology

I think we've adequately covered justification, but just as a refresher...

... if you're using it, you're keeping it.

If you're using it, you're keeping it along with all of its pain. Take another look at your list. Are there any items still marked with a "J"? If so, are you willing to stop using them? If you are, remove the mark now.

If you're not ready to stop using one, accept it, embrace it, and own it. Own the fact that this injury is yours and you're hanging on to it along with its associated pain. There's great power in this because if you own it, you control it, and its destiny is yours to decide.

Now, let's look at the other two reasons we can't forgive. What is it we need?

Justice or an Apology

Why is that? What is it about intentional injuries that absolutely requires one of these two things to happen before we can forgive and let go? Again, we are dealing with *Universal Law*.

To understand this law, we'll start with the tangible laws of science.

I want you to imagine a chair. Now from eighth grade science, what do we know about the matter that makes up this chair? Can we destroy the chair? Can we make it go completely out of existence? If you say, "Yes," I'm calling your eighth grade science teacher right now. The answer is "No." We cannot destroy matter; we can only change its form.

We could beat the chair to bits. We could burn it, etc., but what do we accomplish? We convert its matter to rubble, to dust, or even to energy, but in the end we cannot destroy it. This fundamental truth is helpful in understanding why we can't forgive and let go of the injuries and traumas that have been perpetrated upon us through life.

Once they have been created, *Universal Law* must be satisfied to *un*-create them. Without satisfying *Universal Law* they will exist indefinitely.

When someone commits an act of sin, crime, or offense, something *real* has been created. It is as spiritually real and tangible as the chair. In essence, a contract has been created between the two parties. The offender now *owes* the victim a *debt* of recompense. I call this contract a *"Certificate of Injury."*

Certificate of Injury

This certificate bestows to the Bearer full right to claim just recompense for injuries, pain, and suffering caused by the Grantor.

VALID ONLY TO BEARER

The only way for this contract to be settled is by and through *Universal Law*. Full justice must be measured out upon the offender, or the offender must completely right the wrong they have committed by a true and sincere apology, along with restitution. Let's check in with our own *Inner Truth*. Is this statement true or false? Our *Inner Truth* reveals it to be true.

Without *Universal Law* being satisfied, there is no way to settle the debt, and the consequences upon the offender and the pain of the victim continue.

Can you see how this law creates a very real problem? It requires both parties to create the contract, and it takes both parties to settle it. Since the offender will not make it right and true justice cannot be obtained, this appears to leave us in an impossible situation. *Universal Law* remains unsatisfied, and our own *Inner Truth* has confirmed it.

Fear not! There is a solution to this impossible dilemma.

So where do we turn for relief?

Therapy! "Yup, that'll fix it!" he said sarcastically.

So off we go to therapy to *get fixed*. We talk and talk. We readdress and relive the experience over and over trying to come to terms with or accept it. We learn tricks to try to manage or minimize its effects. Around and around we go until we are finally so darn sick of looking at it and reliving it that we take the injury and stuff it in a drawer to forget about it. Finally, we no longer think about the injury all the time. With therapy now a *"total success,"* we're cured. Right? *Wrong!*

Why are we not cured? Because we are trying to use an emotional or thinking cure on a spiritual injury. As I have said before, I am a strong supporter of the benefits of therapy, but the actual injury at the spirit level (i.e. the bone) has still not been addressed. Forgiveness is the key to healing the spirit.

So what happens the next time we have an injury. We learned in therapy how to stuff it in the drawer so that's what we do. We go over and pull open the drawer to put it in. What happens the moment we open the drawer? We start flipping through all the old injuries. "Oh, I remember this one. Oh yeah, here's this other one I forgot about."

Certificate of Injury

This certificate bestows to the Bearer full right to claim just recompense for injuries, pain, and suffering caused by the Grantor.

VALID ONLY TO BEARER

In other words, the next time we are injured it brings up the pain of past injuries. Why does this occur? The answer is simple. *Universal Law* has not been satisfied, and we still own all our old Certificate's of Injury. Over time we can fill a file cabinet with injuries which we then have to track and manage. We end up with this ledger of unresolved injuries.

I used to own a mortgage company which made and serviced loans. In the beginning it was great. The 1st of every month felt great because it was payday. After a while, however, some loans started to become late or delinquent. Soon I began to dread the 1st day of the month. It was no longer payday but had become "how many late notices" day. The 15th of the month was "eviction or foreclosure notice" day. The 25th of the month was "attorney contact notice" day.

My once fun little business had become my greatest source of irritation and frustration.

One day I was whining to a friend about my misery, and he made a profound suggestion. "Why are you dealing with all this stuff," he said. "Why don't you just hire a collector?"

Ding! Ding! Ding!

Light bulb moment in progress!

Why hadn't I thought of that? Probably because I was so deep in it I could not see the forest through the trees.

So that is exactly what I did. I hired a collection company to handle the accounts, and guess what happened! The 1st of the month was payday again! I didn't concern myself with the collections of the loans any more. I only had to pay attention to the decisions I made so that my business would end up where I wanted it to go.

What would it feel like to no longer hold onto all our injuries? How freeing would that be? What would our ledger look like then?

It would be completely clear, of course.

What if letting go of all the pain and trauma in our own lives could be that easy? What if we could just hire the Ultimate Collector?

Well, guess what? It is just that easy when you know how, and forgiveness is the key.

Again, let's review what forgiveness is *not*. Here are the three major misconceptions we have about forgiveness.

1. Embrace the offender.

We feel that if we forgive, we have to embrace the offender and let them back in. We think somehow true forgiveness means we have to allow them back into our lives.

2. What they did was okay.

It feels like if we forgive them, what we're really

saying is what they did was okay. It sounds ridiculous, but as we have seen it is in the very words we use.

3. We fear that we'll be letting them get away with it.

It feels like if we forgive the offender, we are letting them get away with what they did to us.

None of these things are part of true forgiveness.

Just in case I wasn't clear, let me repeat.

None of these things are required by forgiveness.

Let me give you a true definition of forgiveness.

True forgiveness is no longer holding the offender accountable to us.

Read that a couple more times and let it sink in before moving on. How simple a principle and yet how profound the answer. Is there anything in that definition that says I have to let a dangerous offender back in? Absolutely not! Is there anything in that definition that says what they did was okay? No, there's not. Is there anything in that definition that says they are not accountable or lets them off the hook for their actions? Again, the answer is no.

What if we chose to turn all those Certificates of Injury over to the Ultimate Collector? In my belief system that would be God or Christ. In yours it may be Karma or the Universe, but regardless of the words we use, we all know that what comes around goes around. There is a universal accounting. Our *Inner Truth* tells us this is so.

In my own life, I had to acknowledge that I have no way to obtain justice. I am not able to release the offender from the contract by extending mercy because they have not and will not make it right and the injury remains. Therefore, having no way to settle the painful and traumatic Certificates of Injury I hold, I chose to turn them over to someone or something else for collection. I refused to continue to manage them any longer.

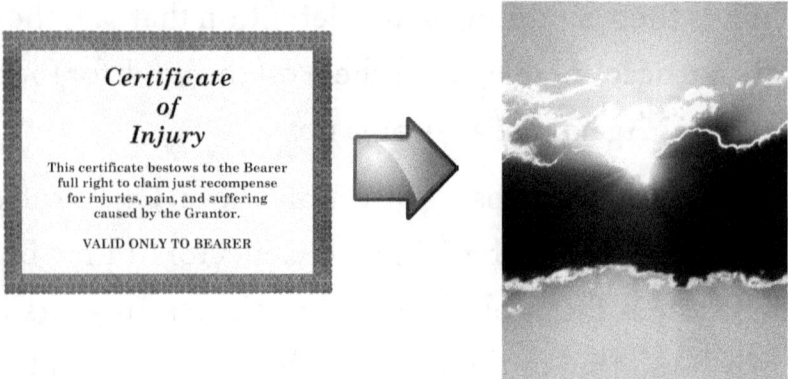

So in the words of my personal belief system, I chose to transfer all my Certificates of Injury to my Lord and Savior, Jesus Christ. He is the only one, according to my belief system, who can measure out true justice upon the offender on my behalf. He is also the only one who can know the heart of a truly penitent offender.

Having failed so many times to handle them myself, I know that the only way the Certificate's I hold can ever be truly collected or settled is by having someone far beyond my own capabilities handle it for me. So that is what I did, and when I did it, something truly miraculous happened. All the associated pain and emotional trauma went with them. My spirit self was whole once again. I was completely free!

Like in the *Give it Back* experience, I didn't ask for or expect all my pain, anger, and hurt to be replaced by peace, calm, and joy. That would be impossible. Right? But the impossible happened anyway!

Do you remember my definition of a miracle? "Something impossible that happens anyway." Like in the *Give it Back* experience, I had given something dark and painful away, and I received a miracle in return.

As a Christian, I have always relied on the promise that as I repent, Jesus takes my sins away and I am saved. In other words, He will take on the responsibility to insure that all the Certificates that I have handed out as the offender (i.e. the debtor) will be satisfied.

We are ever so willing to turn over our debts, but what about when we're the Creditor?

What do we do when we are the holder of someone else's debt? I want you to look closely at the Certificate.

Certificate of Injury

This certificate bestows to the Bearer full right to claim just recompense for injuries, pain, and suffering caused by the Grantor.

VALID ONLY TO BEARER

What does it say right at the bottom?

"VALID ONLY TO BEARER."

If we hold on to our Certificates ourselves, and we do not transfer them to the Collector, does He have any obligation to see that they are settled? Look to your own *Inner Truth* and answer this question for yourself.

So are you ready to be done? Are you willing to never use your injuries as justification again? If so, let's move on.

Chapter 18

The Return

We now have the opportunity to return to our meadow. That safe beautiful place created for you by you. As you read the next section slowly, I want you to remember the meadow that you created and the peace and safety that exist there.

What kind of grass is in your meadow?

Is it long, short, wavy?

Are there wild flowers in your meadow?

Does your meadow have any water?

Is there a pond, lake, river or stream?

Do trees surround your meadow?

What kind of trees are they?

If so, are they pine, oak, pecan, aspen, or ash?

Feel the gentle breeze and allow it to bring to you the smells of your meadow.

Is it woodsy, earthy, floral, or crisp?

What sounds are present in your meadow?

Can you hear the breeze as it passes through the trees?

Are there sounds of wildlife, birds or insects in the distance?

Picture the beautiful blue sky above.

Is it clear, or are there fluffy white clouds floating through the air?

This meadow is safe and completely protected from all danger and harm. Nothing can hurt you in your meadow.

While your meadow re-forms, take a moment to feel the quiet peace that exists in this place.

As quiet peace washes over you, look toward the sky. Again you find that light, that warm peaceful light. This time it's different. Its brightness and intensity are incredible!

It begins to move toward you. This time it moves much faster, and as it enters through the middle of your chest, it explodes out in every direction filling you completely with light and warm radiant peace. The surge of energy is incredible. As you are completely filled with light you become aware that the colors in the meadow are becoming washed out in the white brightness, and you realize that the brightness is emanating from you.

Take a moment and feel the warmth, peace, and security of the meadow. This place is real. You have spiritually created it and you can return here any time you wish.

Now, I want you to turn your attention inside yourself. As you look inside you will again notice the dark spots. These are the traumas and injuries of your life which you are no longer willing to carry. You will not be experiencing or feeling the emotions of these dark spots. Now, I want you to imagine gathering them up, making sure you collect them all.

This is the big stuff. Some of these may be secrets. Things you have never told anyone. Some of these you may have been carrying for a very long time. They are heavy and as you gather them you notice your hands covered in black filth. Leave none behind. Now I want you to imagine holding them out in front of you. You try to compress them down as before, but they just won't get any smaller.

You realize that you have no power over these. Holding them out in front of you again, you will witness the true power available to you. In the words of your own belief system, ask for these things to be taken from you.

As you do, you immediately notice that they begin to get smaller. Smaller and smaller, until they pass from the size of a large grapefruit to a softball, and then a golf ball. They keep getting smaller until they become about the size of a pea. Amazingly, they are still very heavy.

Now, I want you to allow these injuries (all these *Certificates* you have collected over the years), to be transferred from you. As you do, they slowly begin to rise from your hands. The weight lifts away as they ascend slowly into the light. I want you to watch closely as they disappear up into the light. When they are completely gone, look down at your hands. You find that they are completely clean. There is no sign of the filth they once held. Look inside yourself. See the clean space filled with light and void of dark spots.

I want you to again become aware of your meadow. Notice the warm feelings and emotions that come. Enjoy your meadow as long as you like. When you're ready, come back into the awareness of your surroundings.

What you have just experienced is completely unique to you. No one else's experience will be exactly the same as yours.

What happened for you? Were you able to gather up your dark spots? Did you feel the burdens lift as you allowed them to be taken? Take a moment and look at the feelings and emotions you experienced as the healing power of true forgiveness took place. Did you receive a miracle in your life? If so, give thanks in your own way, according to your own belief system. Something *impossible* has just happened anyway!

Occasionally, someone has had a little trouble with this process. In these rare cases, we talk about what may have caused the problem. Sometimes, I have not communicated a point clearly enough, and it has been misunderstood. Almost always though, if something did not resolve, it's because the individual is still using it. They're using it to justify something, or they are just not ready to let it go. If this has happened to you, you have done nothing wrong. You cannot mess this up.

As I have said before, *accept it! Embrace it! Own it!* Own the fact that this injury is yours and you're hanging on to it. There's great power in this because if you own it, you control it, and its destiny is yours to decide.

Take another look at the problem injury to determine how or why you are using, and/or hanging on to it. Again, you didn't mess up! When you're ready, you have the knowledge and tools to be free and let it go.

Now that you have received a miracle in your life and released the injuries that have caused you so much pain and suffering, don't take them back! Today, tomorrow, or sometime soon, the thought is going to come, "No way! It can't be that easy. Was I really healed?" Do not listen! This is a message from the *dark side* that is meant to steal away your new found peace and return you to a life of pain and trauma.

Use the *Give It Back* process to combat these fraudulent thoughts.

The only way you can lose your miracle and return to your former pain is to *take it back* yourself. Do not do this!

With your spirit injuries healed, and the pain and emotional trauma released, we can turn our attention to any residual negative mental or emotional patterns and habits that we may have developed while we were in trauma. This is where a good therapist can make all the difference in the world.

Now that we have let go of the past, we will never get hurt again. Right?

Wrong!

*So, how do we deal with
ongoing and future injuries?
Let's move on to the next chapter and find out.*

Chapter 19

Ongoing and Future Injuries

As long as we are still living and breathing, we are going to get hurt again. Unfortunately, many of the people we must associate with in life are repeat offenders. They may be family, children, an ex-spouse, neighbors, or people from work, church or other groups. They are individuals we cannot avoid in life.

Since we can't rid our lives of these repeat offenders, it can seem like we are stuck in an endless cycle of injury. In addition, new offenders will crop up and hurt us in ways we have not even thought of.

What do we do when new or repeat offenders hurt us? We apply the exact same principles, processes, and tools we have learned throughout this book.

First, we identify the type of injury. If it falls

into the vicarious, incidental or unintentional categories, we can simply choose to let it go and use the *Give It Back* process to eliminate any residual emotions. These types of injuries, if caught early, are very easy to deal with since *Universal Law* does not need to be addressed. With practice in categorizing injuries when they occur, in time you will find that you no longer take these kind of injuries on at all.

Remember, if you have trouble determining whether an injury is intentional or unintentional, always handle it as intentional.

If the category of the new injury is intentional, take the new *Certificate* and transfer it directly onto your *Collector*. With practice, this becomes very natural.

In the live presentation, I have a little demonstration of this process that goes something like this.

I select a member of the audience to give me an injury. I have them say something ridiculous like, "You're the worst speaker ever!" I know, totally preposterous isn't it? Then I have them hand me the corresponding *Certificate of Injury*. As I take the *Certificate*, I show all the pain, hurt, and trauma of the injury on my face and in my posture. I then set the *Certificate* on the table, representing giving it directly to the *Collector*. As I do so, the corresponding relief is clearly evident on my face and in my posture. We repeat the exercise several times.

What do you notice happens in this exercise? Think about this for a moment. What is happening in this simple demonstration?

The injury occurs, and the *Certificate* is received along with its associated emotional pain and suffering. It is then passed on to the *Collector* and its pain and suffering go with it.

But could there be an even better way? Is there a way to avoid the pain and injury all together? How could that be possible? Have you put it together yet?

At this point, we repeat the exercise. The audience member makes the mock offense and attempts to hand me the *Certificate*. This time I refuse to accept it. I simply tell them to pass it directly to the *Collector*. Since I won't take it, the person naturally drops it on the table along with the other *Certificates* already given to the *Collector*. No pain or trauma ever appears in my face or in my posture. Why?

Since I never accepted the injury but, instead, had it given directly to the *Collector*, I didn't receive any of the associated pain or trauma.

This is so simple an idea but the result is astounding.

By mastering the principle of forgiveness and not holding an offender accountable to us, the offender can no longer injure our spirit.

We may have to deal with the outward affects of others actions, but our spirits, hearts, minds, and emotional well-being are no longer available to be played with by others. We no longer take offense. We will never be a victim again!

If we truly understand forgiveness, it will become a state of being and we will never have to address individual injuries again.

When we realize the offenders in our lives
no longer have any power over us,
we receive an unexpected gift.

Chapter 20

The Unexpected Gift

One day I was thinking about a particular offender of mine and an odd thought occurred to me. I kind of felt bad for them. My claim for recompense had gone to the *Ultimate Collector* who could really make that person pay! Over the years I have watched this offender pay and pay for the choices they've made that have hurt others. Now there was one more debt added to the stack.

As I thought of them, I began to feel something that took me completely by surprise. It was warm and gentle, and I could hardly believe I was having *this* feeling associated with *this* person. What I was feeling was compassion. It was honest, sincere compassion.

Now that this person was powerless to hurt me inside, I began to see them in a different way. I saw how they made mistake after mistake. How they couldn't be in a room without lashing out at someone. How their actions left them totally isolated and alone. I saw hopelessness in their eyes and my heart went out to this offender who had hurt me so deeply. As compassion filled my heart, for the first time in my life I truly understood the phrase "*love your enemy.*" I realized that *compassion* is akin to *charity* and in my belief system, and *charity* is the pure *love* of Christ.

I was teaching a lesson on forgiveness to a men's group at my church. I had taught it many times before, but this time, as I prepared, I became very clear on the principles that you have experienced for yourself reading this book. It was eleven days later that my family was killed, and I would put these principles to the ultimate test. I can tell you that they work perfectly. I found, to my surprise, that I never once felt anger, hatred, vengeance, or a need for justice for the individual who killed my family. Amazingly, and exactly as the principles in this book teach, I felt nothing but compassion.

I attended the sentencing of the person responsible for the accident. At any sentencing of this type, the victim's family has the opportunity to speak to the court about the pain and suffering caused by the offender so that it might be considered during sentencing. When that time came, I took my place to address the court. I told the judge that "neither my family or myself harbored any animosity toward the defendant" and asked that the court "be lenient with criminal penalties" and that "we wouldn't request the court take any action on our behalf related to criminal penalties" because we didn't want them or need them. That was it.

I turned and walked back to my chair in the gallery. As the sentencing proceeded, the judge said, "I don't usually get emotional at sentencing, but this is a very difficult situation, and Mr. Howard, I just don't know . . . I agree with you there's just nothing we can do to bring back your family, but frankly your statements have touched me more than anything I've seen since I've been on the bench . . . most people are vindictive, seeking retribution . . . and you, by your statements . . . have made yourself and your family less of a victim . . . you don't have to be a victim the rest of your life. That takes great courage, kindness, and understanding, and it is one of the noblest actions I've seen . . . I apologize." The judge took a moment to regain his composure and, while speaking to the defendant, said, "It's just a tragic circumstance. You'll have repercussions for . . . many years. But, in his expressing his forgiveness, Mr. Howard has touched the court. I think he's also asked for something appropriate to happen. He and his family want to move on and not suffer the rest of their lives as victims, and I think he's also asked that you not become a victim as well."

The judge's statement about my not being a victim had a profound effect on me and has altered the course of my life. I would never be a victim! I knew that was true. I decided I would find a way to pass that on.

After the hearing, I met the family of this individual. Their fear and pain had been evident to me through the short trial. It was a kind and gentle meeting. I then spent about half-an-hour in private talking with the individual one-on-one. I will reserve the content of that visit but I can tell you that the compassion I felt, even with this person in my presence, was substantial and was very evident in our visit and the things we talked about.

I have not seen or spoken to them since. I have often wondered how this individual has fared over the past few years. Perhaps one day I will find out.

Today there are very few offenders in my life. There can be no offender, *to me,* if I *take* no offense (i.e. accept a *Certificate*). Yes, on rare occasion I accept a *Certificate* for a little while, but I become sick of it very quickly and turn it over for collection.

Chapter 21

A Word of Warning

I must give you a word of warning. This is important and, if not heeded, you may find yourself in danger.

Toward the end of one of my live presentations, I overheard a participant say to another something like this. "My husband hasn't hit me in a while. Now that I have forgiven him, I feel like I can let him move back in." I just about flipped out! How could she think an abuser had changed because of her forgiveness?

So let me make this very clear. Forgiveness of others is about you—not them! It changes your heart, heals your spirit, and frees you from the pain and suffering of your injuries. It does nothing for the offender since they have not addressed the requirements of *Universal Law*.

They have not changed. If they were dangerous before, they are dangerous now. If they were a thief before, they are a thief now. If they were an abuser before, that has not changed! You receiving the gift of freedom and compassion does not make a dangerous person safe.

Use wisdom in how you interact with the offenders in your life, so that you and those around you remain safe.

Chapter 22

A Note from the Author

Since I was a boy, it has been one of my deepest desires to make a difference in the world. The knowledge I have attempted to share in this book came at a tremendous personal price. Lives were lost so that I could learn these truths and share them with you. It has been my privilege to be your guide on this journey of personal healing. I hope with all my heart that you have found something that has changed your life. I hope that you have found your own miracle. If you have, then, like me, you now have the opportunity to turn your tragedies to triumph. You too can change the world for good. Follow the desire of your heart to reach out to those you care about and together we will take them on their own journey of healing.

PASS THE MIRACLE ON!

Lifeline Media, LLC hopes you have enjoyed *Overcoming Life's Trauma.*

For more information about products and services visit www.benshoward.com.

Notes

Notes

www.ingramcontent.com/pod-product-compliance
Lightning Source LLC
LaVergne TN
LVHW051839080426
835512LV00018B/2962